# Acknowledgements



The publishers have applied for permission for the following:
*Do Not Be Afraid of the Dark* by Ruskin Bond, *If I Were Brave* by Paro Anand, *Theseus and the Minotaur (http://myths.e2bn.org/index.php).*
Acknowledgements for these texts will be made in the future editions of the book.

Every effort has been made to trace copyright holders and to obtain their permission for the use of copyright material. However, in some instances, we have been unable to trace the owners of the copyright pieces published here. The authors and publishers will gladly receive any information enabling them to rectify any error or omission in subsequent editions.

**Illustrations**
**Cover and Title Page:** Created by Toonfantasy

**Inside: Page 15:** TkKurikawa, Geerati, OscarEspinosa; **16:** pedphoto36pm, belgrafphoto; **17:** DeepGreen; **18:** mammuth; **19:** berdsigns; **20:** Si-Gal; **26:** saifandesign; **28:** Toru-Sanogawa; **29:** piart; **36:** Minaieva; **37:** mammuth; **40:** Big_Ryan; **47:** AlonzoDesign, leremy; **48:** skalapendra, AlonzoDesign; **55:** mammuth; **59:** berdsigns; **76:** StasKhom

# Preface

*Enhanced English Alive* is a multi-skill course in English that adheres to the guidelines laid down by the **National Education Policy, 2020**. This edition retains the original essence of teaching communicative English using a cross-curricular approach and interactive and experiential teaching and learning methods. It offers high-quality English language materials with a coherent structured approach, effective integration of subject knowledge and life skills.

The series comprises Coursebooks and Workbooks for Foundational Stage (Nursery, LKG, UKG, Classes 1 and 2), Preparatory Stage (Classes 3 to 5), and Middle Stage (Classes 6 to 8). Literature Readers are for the Preparatory and Middle Stages (Classes 3 to 8). Each grade package includes a Teacher's Resource Pack and a Collins DigiSuite.

This series integrates the essence of **NIPUN Bharat** guidelines, which extensively deal with foundational literacy and numeracy. Each book aims to motivate learners to read independently, to improve their vocabulary, to develop their critical thinking and creative skills, as well as to enhance their ability to express themselves both verbally and in writing.

This series takes care of the requirements of **Structured Assessments For Analyzing Learning (SAFAL)**. Research-based activities and projects have been used to instill inquiry-based learning, while comprehension passages have been followed by extrapolative and value-based questions that involve analysis-based learning. Additionally, in the Middle Stage (Classes 6 to 8), an end-of-year Assessment Paper has been provided.

## Key features

### Coursebooks

Each Coursebook has a wide variety of texts from genres carefully selected from both Indian and Western literature. The books aim at cross-curricular teaching covering topics included in the syllabus of other subjects taught in the respective grades. They also inculcate mindfulness in learners in the Foundational and Preparatory Stages (Classes 1 to 5), in addition to language skills. A lot of interesting and engaging activities are used as tools to teach language skills.

### Workbooks

The Workbooks have been carefully mapped to the Coursebooks, and created with the intention of independent learning. Each Workbook has 8 comprehension passages including poems.

The vocabulary and grammar sections include a quick recap of the concepts covered in the corresponding chapter of the Coursebook. The listening, speaking, and writing sections allow learners extra practice. Additional assessment papers included in the Workbooks are patterned on the Structured Assessments For Analyzing Learning (SAFAL). These offer a scope for assessing the competencies of critical thinking, inquiry-based learning, and analysis-based learning.

### Literature Readers

- **Reading:** Each book has well-chosen selections from a wide range of literary genres from both Indian and western literature.
- **Summary:** A short summary at the end of each text is provided for an easy way to remember the essence of the text.
- **About the Author:** A short biography, often with images, of authors of the texts in the book, to pique the interests of the learners.

Collins

# Enhanced English Alive

## Literature Reader

# 5

Gunjan Sogani

- **Comprehension:** This section includes exercises including factual, inferential, and extrapolative questions.
- **Vocabulary:** This section teaches new vocabulary including literary devices and is followed by a variety of exercises.
- **Read at Leisure:** A curated list of stories either by the same author or in the same genre to inculcate the spirit of reading in young learners.

## Teacher's Resource Pack

The Teacher's Resource Pack contain model lesson plans, additional worksheets, and grammar based projects covering all the pedagogical aspects included in the Coursebooks, along with listening texts and answer keys to all exercises across Coursebooks, Workbooks, Literature Readers, and additional assessment papers.

# Key to Icons

***Enhanced English Alive*** is a multi-skill course that is closely aligned with the National Education Policy, 2020. It uses an interactive approach, cross-curricular themes, and experiential activities to build communicative competence in students. This series aims to prepare learners with the various skills outlined in the National Education Policy, 2020. These skills have been tagged appropriately with easily recognizable icons for the user's convenience. Here is the key to all the icons used in this series.

## Cross-Curricular Content

- The cross-curricular approach to a topic recognizes that all subjects are interlinked. It includes contributions from several different disciplines or viewpoints for effective learning.
- All chapters have dedicated boxes teaching cross-curricular content appropriate to that class. These boxes cover the following:
  - ***Science Scan*** covers topics related to science.
  - ***Maths Magic*** covers topics related to mathematics.
  - ***Earth Speak*** covers topics related to geography and environmental studies.
  - ***Looking Back*** covers topics related to historical events and personalities.
  - ***Fact File*** covers topics related to general knowledge and awareness.
  - ***Lit Bits*** covers topics related to literature and famous literary figures.
  - ***Art and Culture*** covers topics related to art and culture.

## Twenty-First Century Skills

- The twenty-first century skills ensure that today's students can thrive in an ever-changing world and can use these skills to learn constantly.
- Here are the most commonly cited twenty-first century skills in this series:

Critical Thinking

Communication Skills

Collaboration

Creativity

Information Communication Technology Skills or Digital Literacy

## Experiential Learning

- Experiential learning is a process of learning through hands-on experience. Here, students 'learn by doing' an activity followed by reflective observation on the experience from multiple perspectives.
- This method helps learners link existing knowledge to understand new concepts and apply it to make decisions.

## Art Integration

- Art Integrated Learning (AIL) is a teaching-learning model that integrates fine arts (painting, sculpture, architecture, music, and poetry), performing arts (theatre and dance), and photography with teaching new concepts.
- This provides students with an experiential and a multi-disciplinary learning experience.

## Happiness Content

- Learning should be an enjoyable process for learners. It should focus on building and understanding new concepts rather than rote learning.
- Children should experience happiness through learning and awareness, active participation in class, and also in their relationships with their friends and family.

## India Focus

- India Focus puts spotlight on the heritage, culture, customs, and history and geography of the Indian subcontinent.
- This provides students a deeper understanding of their homeland and creates a sense of solidarity.

## Sustainable Development Goals

- The Sustainable Development Goals, adopted by the United Nations in 2015, are a collection of 17 interlinked global goals designed to achieve a better and more sustainable future for all by 2030. Here are the 17 goals:

# Contents

# 1 The White Elephant

## READING

*Read the story about a great white elephant who lived in the forests of Mount Candorana.*

Once upon a time, there lived a herd of eighty thousand elephants at the foothills of the grand Himalayas. Their leader was a majestic white elephant who was extremely kind-hearted. He loved his blind old mother dearly and took great care of her.

Each day, the white elephant would go deep into the forest in search of the best of wild fruit for his mother. He used to send fruit to his mother through the other elephants in his herd. But they were a bunch of greedy elephants. They used to eat the fruit themselves and never gave anything to the white elephant's old mother. The white elephant was very disappointed with his herd.

One day, he decided to abandon the herd, and go with his mother to Mount Candorana to live in a cave beside a beautiful lake that had lovely pink lotuses.

It so happened one day that a forester from Banaras lost his way in the forest and was absolutely terrified to find himself alone in the thick woods. He was weeping bitterly and desperately looking to find some help. The white elephant took pity on the man and promised to help him. He knew every inch of that dense forest and showed him the way

majestic: grand; impressive because of size or beauty
abandon: to leave a place, thing, or person with no intention of returning
terrified: badly scared
desperately: with great need or urgency

out to Banaras city. The forester thanked the white elephant before leaving for home happily.

While passing through the bustling streets of Banaras a few days later, the forester heard an announcement: 'Listen, everyone! King Brahamadutta's favourite elephant has left for his heavenly abode. Our king is now looking for a new elephant to take his beloved elephant's place. Anyone who knows of an elephant fit for the king's palace should approach the court. He will be rewarded handsomely!' The forester thought, 'If I tell the king about the magnificent white elephant of Mount Candorana, I will certainly be rewarded by the king!' He had obviously forgotten how kind the elephant had been to him and promptly went to the royal court. Appearing before the king, he said, 'My Lord! I know of a very good elephant that would be suitable for you!'

'Where can we find him?' asked the king.

The forester told the king that the white elephant lived in Mount Candorana. The king decided to go in search of that white elephant the very next day.

bustling: full of people moving about in a busy way
abode: the place where you live
magnificent: extremely good and beautiful

The next morning, even before the sun had risen, the forester led the king and his men to the place where the white elephant lived. When the white elephant saw the forester, he realised that it was he who had led the king's men to him. He was very upset about the man's selfishness and ingratitude. He decided not to put up a fight because he didn't want to harm anyone. So, he went peacefully with the king and his men to the city of Banaras.

When the white elephant did not return home, his mother was very worried. She had heard all the commotion and guessed that the king's men must have taken her son away. She lay down in her cave and cried bitterly.

Meanwhile, the white elephant was led to the beautiful city of Banaras, where he was given a grand reception in the royal elephant shed. The mahout had laid out a feast for him and decorated the shed with fragrant flowers. But the elephant neither touched the food, nor seemed to be impressed with the beautiful and comfortable shed. He just sat there with a woeful expression on his face. He was thinking of his mother and how sad she would be without him.

The matter was reported to the king. 'Your Highness, the new elephant refuses to eat or drink anything that we have given him,' said the mahout. The king was disturbed by the news. He decided to visit the shed and see for himself what the matter was.

On reaching the shed, the king asked the white elephant, 'Dear friend, what ails you? Are you not happy being here with us?' The white elephant replied, 'Your Highness, I thank you for all your love and kindness, and I couldn't ask for better treatment. But I have left my

ingratitude: the state of not being thankful
commotion: a lot of noise, confusion, and excitement
mahout: a person who works with and cares for an elephant

blind old mother in the forest. She will die without me. I request you to release me so that I can return to the forest and look after her.'

The **compassionate** king was touched by the elephant's story. He replied gently, 'Oh! I didn't know that. Of course, you must return to your mother and take care of her.'

The elephant was overjoyed. 'I cannot thank you enough, Your Highness! My mother will be so happy when I go back to her,' he cried.

As soon as he was released, the elephant ran back to his home as fast as he could. His mother immediately recognised the scent of her son and was overjoyed to have him back. She prayed to God to bless the kind king with peace, **prosperity**, and happiness.

The white elephant took good care of his mother till the day she died. The king often visited him in the forest. And when the white elephant himself died, the king built a statue of him by the lake and held an annual elephant festival there in his memory.

**compassionate:** feeling or showing sympathy for those who are suffering
**prosperity:** the state of being successful, especially in making money

## SUMMARY

The white elephant and his blind mother lived peacefully in a forest. One day the white elephant helps a forester, who, in turn, betrays him and tells the king about him. When the king gets to know about the beautiful elephant, he wants the animal for himself. Now, the elephant lives in the king's shed, but is extremely unhappy because his mother is alone in the forest. When the king gets to know about the reason behind the elephant's unhappiness, he lets him go back to his old mother. The elephant and his mother are reunited in the end. The king and the elephant continue to be friends. When the elephant dies, the king builds a statue in his memory.

## About the Genre

*Jataka Tales* were written around 300 BC and have been passed on from generation to generation. These tales of wisdom serve as guidance on moral behaviour for us. The tales are mainly about the life of Lord Buddha and are meant to teach us values like self-sacrifice, truth, honesty, and kindness.

# COMPREHENSION

**A. Mark the sentences as true (T) or false (F).**

1. A herd of eighty thousand animals lived at the foothills of the Himalayas. ☐
2. The white elephant's mother was lame. ☐
3. The white elephant left his herd because he was disappointed with their dishonest behaviour. ☐
4. The forester lost his way in the jungle one day. ☐
5. The white elephant went with the king because he was scared. ☐
6. The king did not want to let the white elephant return to his mother. ☐

**B. Read the descriptions and say whom they describe.**

| | |
|---|---|
| 1. He was a majestic animal. He loved his mother very much and took great care of her. He did not want to harm anyone. | ............................................ |
| 2. They were greedy and selfish. They took something that was meant for a poor old elephant and ate it up themselves. | ............................................ |
| 3. He was ungrateful and selfish. He cheated an animal that had helped him when he needed it. | ............................................ |
| 4. He was a kind person. He was a good listener and a friend. He was a true leader. | ............................................ |
| 5. She was blind and helpless. She truly loved her son and was broken-hearted when he was taken away from her. | ............................................ |

**C. Answer the questions briefly.**

1. Where did the white elephant live at the beginning of the story and with whom?
2. Why did the white elephant leave his herd?
3. How did the white elephant help the forester?
4. Why did the forester tell the king about the white elephant? What does it tell us about him?
5. The white elephant goes away peacefully with the king and his men. Why does he do so? What quality does he show by doing so?
6. How did the king and the elephant continue their friendship even after the elephant returned to his mother?

**D. Think and answer the questions.**

1. If you could change the ending of the story, how would you end the story? Describe the ending.
2. Give the story an alternate title. Explain why you chose that title.
3. *Jataka Tales* teach us values. What value do you think this story teaches us?

## VOCABULARY

**A. Circle the odd word in each set.**

| 1. | grand | majestic | magnificent | shabby |
|---|---|---|---|---|
| 2. | dishonest | greedy | selfish | thirsty |
| 3. | abandon | accept | receive | welcome |
| 4. | aggressive | quiet | violent | wild |
| 5. | compassionate | harsh | kind | thoughtful |
| 6. | poverty | prosperity | riches | wealth |
| 7. | cheerful | grim | woeful | miserable |
| 8. | lively | bustling | inactive | thriving |
| 9. | scent | stink | fragrance | incense |
| 10. | abode | residence | home | inn |

B. **The king lived in a *palace*, and the elephant lived inside a *cave* in a jungle. Do you know what people around the world call their homes? Unscramble the names of the homes given below. You can use an encyclopedia or the Internet for help.**

1. This is a traditional Korean house.

   ..........................................

   (KONAH)

2. This is a temporary winter shelter built by Inuit hunters for their families before going on a hunting trip.

   ..........................................

   (GOLIO)

3. This is a traditional Indonesian house. It has a huge, boat-shaped roof.

   ..........................................

   (NANOKGNOT)

4. This is a traditional Chinese house. This house has a courtyard surrounded by buildings on all sides.

   ......................................

   (ANUYEHIS)

5. These are conical tents made of skins, cloth, or canvas on a frame of poles. It originated in North America.

   ......................................

   (TEEEP)

*Read at leisure...*

- Stories from *Jataka Tales*
- *Indian Folk-Tales and Legends* by Pratibha Nath
- *Indian Folktales* by Anupa Lal

# 2 Do Not Be Afraid of the Dark

## READING

*Are you afraid of the dark? What scares you when it is dark? Read the poem to find out what the poet tells us to do at night.*

Don't be afraid of the dark, little one,
The earth must rest when the day is done.
The sun must be harsh, but moonlight—never!
And those stars will be shining forever and ever,

Be friends with the Night, there is nothing to fear,
Just let your thoughts travel to friends far and near.
By day, it does seem that our troubles won't cease,
But at night, late at night, the world is at peace.

*–Ruskin Bond*

harsh: unpleasant or rough
cease: to stop
at peace: calm and relaxed; in a state of harmony or friendship

## SUMMARY

In the poem, the poet encourages a young child to not be afraid of the dark. Night is the time when the earth needs to rest in the gentle light of the moon and the stars. The poet suggests that the child be friends with the night and think of her dear ones when it gets dark. It may seem that our problems will never end, but night brings peace and rest from the worries of the day.

## About the Poet

**Ruskin Bond**, an Indian author of British origin, is one of the most popular children's writers in India. The author began writing his first novel, *The Room on the Roof*, at the age of 17. He also won the John Llewellyn Rhys Memorial Prize for this work. He has also been rewarded with other prestigious awards, such as the Sahitya Akademi Award in 1992 and the Padma Shri in 1999.

# COMPREHENSION

**A. Answer the questions briefly.**

1. Who is the poet talking to in the poem? How do you know?
2. Why, according to the poet, do we have nights?
3. How can we overcome fear?
4. When is the 'world at peace'?
5. Pick out the pairs of rhyming words from the poem.
6. Find information about a well-known person who faced fear bravely. Describe what the person did.

**B. Read these lines from the poem and answer the questions.**

1. *The sun must be harsh, but moonlight—never!*
   *And those stars will be shining forever and ever*

   a. How does the poet describe the sunlight and the moonlight?

   b. For how long will the stars shine?

2. *By day, it does seem that our troubles won't cease,*
   *But at night, late at night, the world is at peace.*

a. How do things seem during the day?

b. What does the poet mean by *the world is at peace*?

**C. Read the poem once more. Now, tick (✓) the statements you agree with, and cross (X) the ones you don't agree with. Then, discuss each statement with your teacher.**

1. We are more relaxed during the day than at night. ☐
2. The stars represent hope that stays with us forever. ☐
3. We must not let problems scare us. ☐
4. Our family and friends help us in difficult times. ☐
5. We must never lose hope. ☐

## VOCABULARY

### Alliteration

- Read this line from the poem.

  *The earth must rest when the day is done.*

  The poet uses a poetic device called alliteration in *the day is done.*

- **Alliteration** occurs when two or more words that are close together begin with the same sound.
- Alliteration gives a musical rhythm to a poem and makes it easier to recite. For example:

  *Three grey geese in a green field grazing.*

  *Betty bought some butter, but the butter was bitter.*

  *The gentle giant jumped with joy.*

**Add words from the box to create alliteration in each sentence.**

*busy teacher slept hurried song pounced*
*mouthwatering clean deep seashells*

1. I ........................ home to do my homework.
2. The ................................. bees went buzzing busily.

3. Cathy, come and ................................... your cupboard.
4. Sonia sang a silly ...................................
5. Dinesh dived ................................... into the sea.
6. Peter ................................... and picked the poppies in the garden.
7. Martha's mother makes ................................... muffins.
8. The ................................... asked Tim to tell a tale.
9. Sanya sells ................................... on the seashore.
10. The slithery snake ................................... silently.

*Read at leisure...*

- *Great Stories for Children* by Ruskin Bond
- *The Blue Umbrella* by Ruskin Bond
- *All-Time Favourites for Children* by Ruskin Bond

# 3 If I Were Brave

## READING

*Are you a brave child? Or are you mostly scared? Read this story about a boy who fears everything under the sun!*

I am scared of everything. My sister says, 'You could make a dictionary of all the things you're scared of.'

A for Accidents
B for Bullies
C for Caterpillars
D for Dogs
E for Elevators
F for Fire
G for Gangsters
H for Heights
I for Injuries
J for Jumping down the stairs
K for Knives (sharp ones)
L for Lizards
M for Mummy's anger
N for the Night
O for Oceans (or any big body of water)
P for Pain
Q for Questions in class
R for Report card

**gangsters:** members of a group of criminals
**injuries:** cuts on the body due to an accident or an attack

S for Snakes (lots of people are scared, but I'm petrified)
T for Tests (ditto)
U for Ugly things
V for Vaccinations
W for Weather (the thunder and lightning kind)
X for X-files (and other scary programs)
Y for Yawning (I'm scared of lock jaw)
Z for Zoos

Actually, my whole life is spent in being frightened of things and worrying when anyone tries to do anything even remotely scary. It's always been like that and… I'm afraid… it will always be like that.

Then one day, the family went for a picnic by the side of a lake. There was swimming and parasailing. Everyone was having a great time, except me, of course. I was in a rotten mood. Everyone else cooled off in the water. My littlest cousins, Angad and Neha, slapped the water gleefully; the teens set off to the far end for parasailing. The grown-ups decided on an afternoon nap and went up to the cottage they had hired. That left me, and my sulky self, sitting on the beach. I'd finished the book I was reading. I watched the brats playing and sometime later, I fell asleep.

Water surrounded me on all sides. I struggled to get a breath. Something was pulling me back into the water, I gasped. I was dying. 'Help me! Get up and help me!' I moaned.

And the moaning went on and on. 'Help me!' But it wasn't my voice. I surfaced from my sleep, dazed to find Angad shaking me, sobbing, 'Help me, get up and help me!'

'Wh-what?' I sat up. Angad was already running to the water's edge, shouting. Something, far out, almost in the middle of the lake, was splashing. It was Neha. She was drowning.

I looked around. There was no one else around. No one except me. But, I couldn't swim. I was scared of water. 'HELP!' I shouted, but there was

vaccinations: medicines given through injection to prevent people from getting a disease
lock jaw: a condition which makes your jaw muscles stiff
parasailing: a sport in which a water-skier wears a parachute and is towed by a speedboat
gleefully: happily
sulky: someone who is unwilling to enjoy himself/herself
surfaced: rose

no one to hear, '*Hurry, hurry*,' coaxed Angad. There was only one way out, only one way. Neha's life was in my hands, literally.

I grabbed Angad's tube. It was a bit small, but I couldn't swim, so there was no way I could do without it. 'Angad, go call the grown-ups, tell them to hurry. GO!' I shouted as he gaped at me. I stepped into the water. There was no time to feel the cold, there was no time for fear as my feet left the safety of the sandy floor and began to tread on water. I was surrounded by it. This was my worst nightmare coming true.

'Help me! Help me!' sobbed Neha as I neared her. Her head bobbed above the surface of the water for a brief moment and then disappeared. I splashed harder. I felt around under the water, but I couldn't feel Neha anywhere. The water was murky, I couldn't see her either. Swallowing the hard lump of my fear, I put my face into the water. I choked. No, I couldn't. I couldn't go under water. I kicked about with my legs—no Neha. I realised that I was crying.

I felt something close around my ankle, a hand. She was pulling me down. And down I went, the water closing over me. I don't quite know how I did it. But one moment, my little sister and I were on our way down, down, down. Then I managed to grab the hand that held my foot. As soon as I had a firm grip, I turned my face up towards the murky light, lungs bursting for air. Up and up. I broke through the water gasping. But Neha still hadn't come up. With an almighty yank on the little hand, I forced her face out of the water.

Then my arms went around her waist and held on tight, crying. All the strength suddenly draining out of me. I couldn't make it back. I just couldn't. I just held her and she hung limply in my arms. Her head lolling backwards, her eyes closed. *But I had to get her back…*

Soon we were back… safe, dry land. Neha was alive. Shaken, but alive. And so was I.

coaxed: gently tried to persuade someone to do something
literally: actually
gaped: looked at someone with surprise
tread: put your foot on something
murky: too dark and dirty to see through
almighty: very great
draining: empty out
lolling: hanging loosely

I was suddenly a big hero. I was suddenly brave, congratulated and feted by all. But it's not as if I got over my alphabetical list of fears. I'm still scared of things. I'm even more scared of drowning and water than ever before. But, I guess, as Ma says, I overcame my fear when it mattered most. Even if I'm not as brave as others, I guess that I'm as brave as myself and that's good enough for me.

feted: honoured

*(An abridged version of a story by Paro Anand)*

## SUMMARY

The narrator of the story is a child, and he is scared of all things that can be imagined. He has a long alphabetical list of things he fears. One day, the boy's family goes for a picnic by a lake. The boy is left alone with his little cousins. While the little children play in the water, the boy falls asleep reading a book. He wakes up to his cousin Angad crying for help—Neha is drowning. The narrator does not know how to swim, yet he jumps into the water and saves the girl. He realises that he may not be brave as others, but he is certainly brave when it matters the most.

## About the Author

**Paro Anand** is an Indian author who writes for all age groups. Her initiative, *Literature in Action*, holds the world record for making the world's longest newspaper. Over three thousand children worked on it from 16 states in 10 different languages. She speaks several languages, and has also won the Bal Sahitya Puraskar.

## COMPREHENSION

**A. Fill in the blanks.**

1. The child feels that he isn't .................................. like others.
2. The child's sister feels that he can make a .................................. of all the things he is scared of.
3. The child's family went on a .................................. one day.
4. The child had a .................................. while he slept.
5. .................................. woke the child because .................................. was drowning in the lake.
6. The child is honoured as a .................................. after he saved his cousin from drowning.

**B. Read these sentences and say who could have said these lines in the story.**

1. Everything scares me. ..........................................
2. I just don't feel like swimming. ..........................................
3. Help me save Neha! ..........................................
4. I won't let you drown! ..........................................
5. Thank you for saving my life! ..........................................
6. You were brave when it mattered the most. ..........................................

**C. Answer the questions briefly.**

1. What does the scared child wish for?
2. What is the child most scared of by the end of the story? Why do you think it scares him so much?
3. Describe how the child saves his cousin from drowning.

**D. Think and answer the questions.**

1. The child thinks that he isn't a brave boy. Do you also think that? Give reasons to support your answer.
2. In the end the child says, 'I'm as brave as myself and that's good enough for me'. What does he mean by this?
3. Write about your biggest fear. How do you think you can overcome it?

## VOCABULARY

**A. Read the definitions and complete the words from the story.**

1. Dark and so dirty that you can't look through it:

   MU .......... .......... ..........

2. A short breath of air you take in through your mouth:

   GA .......... ..........

3. A dream that is frightening:

   NI .......... .......... .......... .......... .......... .......... ..........

4. To look at someone or something in wonder with one's mouth open wide: GA .......... ..........

5. Ready to face danger:

   BR .......... .......... ..........

6. Crying noisily:

   SO .......... .......... .......... .......... ..........

**B. The child's family went on a picnic by the lake. Find ten picnic/beach words in the word grid.**

| S | U | N | G | L | A | S | S | E | S |
|---|---|---|---|---|---|---|---|---|---|
| A | H | M | J | K | L | P | O | U | G |
| N | V | D | F | T | Y | A | H | J | T |
| D | R | E | W | Y | S | D | T | B | D |
| C | H | M | T | R | M | E | K | L | O |
| A | B | X | C | R | A | B | F | A | L |
| S | E | A | S | H | E | L | L | N | P |
| T | X | C | W | N | M | A | S | K | H |
| L | Q | T | I | Y | U | P | I | E | I |
| E | W | R | M | H | S | K | L | T | N |

*Read at leisure...*

- *Taranauts* by Roopa Pai
- *Grandma's Bag of Stories* by Sudha Murthy
- *Excuses, Excuses* by Anushka Ravishankar

# 4 Christmas Won

## READING

*Read a story about four sisters and how they celebrate Christmas when their father is away at war.*

**Characters**

- ***Meg:*** Eldest sister, sixteen years old
- ***Jo:*** Second sister, fifteen years old
- ***Beth:*** Third sister, thirteen years old
- ***Amy:*** Youngest sister, twelve years old
- ***Mrs March:*** Mother of Meg, Jo, Beth, and Amy

*Four sisters sit knitting while the December snow falls quietly outside, and the fire crackles cheerfully within. It is a comfortable room, though the carpet is faded and the furniture very plain. The girls are waiting for their mother to arrive home.*

**Jo:** *[grumbling]* Christmas won't be Christmas without any presents.

**Meg:** It's so terrible to be poor!

**Amy:** I don't think it's fair for some girls to have plenty of pretty things, and other girls, nothing at all.

**Beth:** We've got Father and Mother, and each other.

*The four young faces brightened at the cheerful words, but darkened again thinking of their father far away, where the war was being fought.*

**Jo:** *[sadly]* We haven't got Father and shall not have him for a long time.

*Nobody spoke for some time.*

**Meg:** You know the reason Mother said we shouldn't have any presents this Christmas was because it is going to be a hard winter for everyone; and she thinks we shouldn't spend money for pleasure when our men are suffering in the army. We can't do much, but we can make our little sacrifices, and we should do it gladly.

**Jo:** But I don't think the little we should spend would do any good. We've each got a dollar, and the army wouldn't be much helped by our giving that. I agree not to expect anything from you or Mother, but I do want to buy some books for myself.

**Beth:** I planned to spend mine on new music.

**Amy:** I shall get a nice box of Faber's drawing pencils. I really need them.

**Jo:** Mother didn't say anything about our money, and she won't wish us to give up everything. Let's each buy what we want and have a little fun. I'm sure we work hard enough to earn it.

**Meg:** *[complaining]* I know I do—teaching those tiresome children nearly all day, when I'm longing to enjoy myself at home.

**Jo:** You don't have half such a hard time as I do. How would you like to be shut inside a room for hours with a nervous, fussy old lady, who keeps you trotting?

**Beth:** *[with a sigh]* It's not nice to complain so much, but I do think washing dishes and keeping things tidy is the worst work in the

darkened: (here) felt unhappy
tiresome: boring or annoying
fussy: someone who is difficult to please
trotting: moving fast

world. It makes me cross, and my hands get so stiff, I can't practice well at all.

**Amy:** I don't believe any of you suffer as I do, for you don't have to go to school with impertinent girls, who tease you if you don't know your lessons, and laugh at your dresses, and say that your father isn't rich, and insult you when your nose isn't nice.

*So, the girls continued talking... The clock struck six. Beth put a pair of slippers down to warm next to the fireplace. Somehow, the sight of the old shoes had a good effect upon the girls, for Mother was coming, and everyone brightened to welcome her. Meg lit the lamp, Amy got out of the easy chair without being asked, and Jo forgot how tired she was as she sat up to hold the slippers nearer to the fire.*

**Jo:** They are quite worn out. Marmee must have a new pair.

**Beth:** I thought I'd get her some with my dollar.

**Amy:** No, I shall!

**Meg:** I'm the oldest...

**Jo:** *[speaking quickly]* I'm the man of the family now that Papa is away, and I shall provide the slippers for he told me to take special care of Mother while he was gone.

**Beth:** I'll tell you what we'll do, let's each get her something for Christmas and not get anything for ourselves.

**Jo:** *[excitedly]* What will we get?

*Everyone thought for a minute.*

**Meg:** I shall give her a nice pair of gloves.

**Jo:** Army shoes, best to be had.

**Beth:** Some handkerchiefs.

**Amy:** I'll get a little bottle of perfume. She likes it, and it won't cost much, so I'll have some left to buy my pencils.

impertinent: rude or disrespectful
worn out: old or in a poor condition
Marmee: (here) Mother; the March sisters call their mother *Marmee*

**Meg:** How will we give the things?

**Jo:** Put them on the table, and bring her in, and see her open the bundles. Don't you remember how we used to do on our birthdays?

**Beth:** Yes, let Marmee think we are getting things for ourselves, and then surprise her. We must go shopping tomorrow afternoon.

*At this moment, the door opens, and mother walks in. Mrs March is not elegantly dressed, but is a noble-looking woman. To her children, she is the most splendid woman in the world.*

**Mrs March:** Glad to find you so merry, my girls. Has anyone called, Beth? How is your cold, Meg? Jo, you look tired. Come and hug your mother, baby.

*Mrs March gets her wet things off, her warm slippers on, and sitting down in the easy chair, drew Amy to her lap. The girls flew about, trying to make things comfortable for her.*

**Mrs March:** I've got a treat for you after supper.

**Beth:** A letter! A letter! Three cheers for Father!

**Mrs March:** *[patting her pocket]* Yes, a nice long letter. He is well, and thinks he shall get through the cold season better than we feared. He sends all sorts of loving wishes for Christmas, and a special message to you girls.

**Beth:** I think it was so splendid of Father to go as a chaplain when he was too old to be sent as a soldier.

**Jo:** *[with a groan]* Don't I wish I could go as a drummer or a nurse, so I could be near him and help him!

**Amy:** It must be very unpleasant to sleep in a tent, and eat all sorts of bad-tasting things, and drink out of a tin mug.

**Beth:** When will he come home, Marmee?

elegantly: stylishly
noble-looking: respected and admired
splendid: very good
chaplain: someone who does religious work in hospitals, schools, or in the army
unpleasant: something that makes you feel uncomfortable or unhappy

**Mrs March:** Not for many months, dear, unless he is sick. He will stay and do his work faithfully as long as he can, and we won't ask for him back a minute sooner than he can be spared. Now come and hear the letter.

*They all drew to the fire, Mrs March in the big chair with Beth at her feet, Meg and Amy perched on either arm of the chair, and Jo leaning on the back, where no one would see any sign of emotion if the letter should happen to be touching.*

*It was a cheerful letter, full of descriptions of camp life, marches, and military news. Towards the end, it overflowed with fatherly love for the little girls at home.*

**Mrs March:** *[reading the letter]* 'Give them all my dear love and a kiss. Tell them I think of them every day and pray for them at night. A year seems very long to wait before I see them, but remind them that while we wait, we may all work, so that these hard days need not be wasted. I know they will remember all I said to them, that they will be loving children to you, will do their duty faithfully, fight their bosom enemies bravely, and conquer themselves so beautifully that

spared: made free
touching: (here) making you feel emotional
bosom: (here) close

when I come back to them I may be fonder and prouder than ever of my little women.'

**Amy:** *[crying]* I am a selfish girl! But I'll truly try to be better, so he may not be disappointed in me.

**Meg:** We all will. I think too much of my looks and hate to work, but won't any more, if I can help it.

**Jo:** I'll try and not be rough and wild, but do my duty here instead of wanting to be somewhere else.

*Beth said nothing, but wiped away her tears with the blue army sock and began to knit with all her might, losing no time in doing the duty that lay nearest her, while she determined to be all that Father hoped to find her when the year brought round the happy homecoming.*

*That night, they sang, as usual, before they went to bed. Meg had a voice like a flute, and she and Mrs March led the little choir. Amy chirped like a cricket, and Jo sang at her own sweet will. This was a common custom at their house. Mrs March was a wonderful singer, and the girls never grew too old for their familiar lullaby.*

determined: made up your mind to do something
lullaby: a song that is sung to little children to help them fall asleep

## SUMMARY

Beth, Amy, Jo, and Meg are sisters. Their father is a chaplain and he is away at war. It is Christmas time and they each have a dollar. While waiting for their mother to return from work, they all think of what to buy for themselves. However, they soon realise that they should be buying something for their mother instead as most of her things are old and worn out. They selflessly decide what gifts to buy for their mother. When Mrs March returns, they all read a letter from their father. Their father asks them to be brave and continue to do their duties faithfully.

## About the Author

**Louisa May Alcott** (1832–1888) was an American writer. She started working at a very young age, and her jobs included working as a governess, a teacher, and a domestic helper. Initially, she published many stories and novels under a different name. However, she used her own name for the novel, *Little Women*, which is her most famous work. This book was so successful that Alcott became a full-time writer. She also wrote *Good Wives*, *Little Men*, *Eight Cousins* and *Jo's Boys*.

## COMPREHENSION

**A. Who says the following lines in the play?**

1. It's so terrible to be poor!
2. I do want to buy some books for myself.
3. It's not nice to complain so much, but I do think washing dishes and keeping things tidy is the worst work in the world.
4. I'll get a little bottle of perfume.
5. He will stay and do his work faithfully as long as he can.
6. Tell them I think of them every day and pray for them at night.

**B. Choose the correct option.**

1. Out of the four sisters, .......................................... is the youngest.
   a. Amy
   b. Beth
   c. Jo
2. The girls can't buy Christmas presents because ........................................................
   a. their father is at war.
   b. they are very poor.
   c. it is war time, and they shouldn't be spending money for pleasure.
3. The girls' father is a .............................. in the army.
   a. general
   b. chaplain
   c. soldier
4. .............................. wants to buy herself some music for Christmas.
   a. Amy
   b. Jo
   c. Beth
5. Mrs March tells the girls that she has got .............................. for them.
   a. Christmas gifts
   b. a letter from their father
   c. good news

**C. Answer the questions briefly.**

1. What are the girls talking about at the beginning of the play?
2. Where is the girls' father?
3. What kind of work does Meg do?
4. What do the girls decide to buy for their mother for Christmas? What does it tell you about them?
5. What does the father want the girls to do while he is away at war?
6. What does Beth do after hearing out the letter?

**D. Think and answer these questions.**

1. Write down all the words you can think to describe Mrs March in the word web given below. Discuss briefly why you think she has these qualities.

2. In his letter, the father asks his daughters to work hard and be better than they already are. Suggest two ways in which you can improve yourself.
3. In the play, the girls try to make their mother comfortable. Talk about a few things you do to help your parents at home.

## VOCABULARY

### Phrasal verbs

- Read these sentences from the play.

  *They are quite worn out. Marmee must have a new pair.*

  Here, *worn out* means *old*. *Worn out* is a phrasal verb.

- A **phrasal verb** is a combination of a verb with an adverb or a preposition.
- The addition of the adverb or preposition to the verb changes the meaning of the verb. For example:

  *The party was called off.*

  Here, *called off* means *cancelled.*

  *They kept on working.*

  Here, *kept on* means *continued.*

**A. Match these phrasal verbs with their meanings.**

| Phrasal Verb | Meaning |
|---|---|
| 1. break down | a. to eat at a restaurant |
| 2. come forward | b. to stop working |
| 3. dress up | c. to become an adult |
| 4. eat out | d. to offer to do something |
| 5. give away | e. to wear nice clothes |
| 6. grow up | f. to give something to someone for free |

**B. Make sentences with the phrasal verbs you just learnt.**

1. ..............................................................................................................
   ..............................................................................................................
2. ..............................................................................................................
   ..............................................................................................................
3. ..............................................................................................................
   ..............................................................................................................
4. ..............................................................................................................
   ..............................................................................................................
5. ..............................................................................................................
   ..............................................................................................................
6. ..............................................................................................................
   ..............................................................................................................

*Read at leisure...*

- *Eight Cousins* by Louisa May Alcott
- *Christmas Treats* by Enid Blyton
- *Charlie and the Chocolate Factory* by Roald Dahl

# 5 Something Told the Wild Geese

## READING

*Have you ever seen a flock of birds flying away together? Where do you think they are going? Read the poem to find out why the wild geese leave the beautiful golden fields behind.*

**Literary device**

Refrain is a word, group of words, line, or group of lines repeated many times. For example: *Something told the wild geese; Something whispered, 'snow'.*

Something told the wild geese
It was time to go.
Though the fields lay golden
Something whispered, 'snow'.

Leaves were green and stirring,
Berries, luster-glossed.
But beneath warm feathers
Something cautioned, 'frost'.

All the sagging orchards
Steamed with amber spice.
But each wild breast stiffened
At remembered ice.

Something told the wild geese
It was time to fly,
Summer sun was on their wings,
Winter in their cry.

*–Rachel Field*

cautioned: warned about problems or danger
frost: a weather condition when the temperature falls below freezing point, and the ground is covered in ice crystals
sagging: drooping or hanging down
amber: (here) yellowish-brown colour
stiffened: stopped moving and became tense in fear or anger

## SUMMARY

The poem is about a flock of wild geese that flies to a different place when the weather gets cold. The poet says that something tells the wild geese that it will soon snow even when the fields are golden with sunlight. The leaves may still be green, and the trees might be full of fruit, but the flock can sense the beginning of winter and fly away to warm places.

### About the Poet

**Rachel Field** (1894–1942) was an American novelist and poet. She wrote for both adults and children. Some of her most popular poetry collections for children include *Taxis and Toadstools*, *An Alphabet for Boys and Girls*, and *A Circus Garland: Poems*. She was a well-known playwright too, and her plays include *Cinderella Married, A Comedy in One Act* and *The Bad Penny: A Drama in One Act*. She also wrote the English lyrics for Franz Schubert's *Ave Maria*, which was used in the 1940 Disney film *Fantasia*.

## COMPREHENSION

**A. Answer the questions briefly.**

1. Who is the poet talking about in the poem?
2. What is the colour of the leaves and the fields in the poem?
3. What do you think the poet means by these phrases?
   a. *luster-glossed*
   b. *green and stirring*
4. What do the birds remember? How do they react to it?
5. The poet refers to two seasons in the poem—summer and winter. Which words does she use to refer to them? Find them and put them into the correct columns.

| Summer | Winter |
|---|---|
| | |
| | |
| | |
| | |

**B. Read the lines from the poem and answer the questions.**

1. *But beneath warm feathers*
   *Something cautioned, 'frost'.*
   a. Who has *warm feathers*?
   b. Why are their feathers warm?
   c. What warning do they get?

2. *All the sagging orchards*
   *Steamed with amber spice.*
   a. Why are the orchards sagging?
   b. What is *amber spice*?
   c. What does the poet mean by *steamed*?

**C. Think and answer the questions.**

1. What natural phenomenon is taking place in the poem?
2. The poet uses the word *something* many times in the poem. Who or what do you think is *something*? Give a reason for your answer.
3. What does the poet mean when she says, 'Summer sun was on their wings'? How would you write this line if it were a cloudy or a rainy day?

## VOCABULARY

### Adjectives

Read the poem again. Did you notice how the poet has used adjectives to make things seem more real to us? For example:

*wild* geese
*sagging* orchards
*luster-glossed* berries
*warm* feathers
*golden* fields
*amber* spice
*wild* breast

Match the adjectives in Column A with the words in Column B to make meaningful pairs. Compare your list with your partner.

| Column A | Column B |
|---|---|
| 1. cruel | a. apples |
| 2. fast | b. asleep |
| 3. loud | c. mistake |
| 4. sun-kissed | d. music |
| 5. tasteless | e. summer |
| 6. terrible | f. winters |

*Read at leisure...*

- *The Playhouse Key* by Rachel Field
- *A Bird Came Down the Walk* by Emily Dickinson
- *The Owl* by Alfred Tennyson

# 6 Theseus and the Minotaur

## READING

*The Minotaur was a monster, half bull and half human, in Greek mythology. He lived in the labyrinth, which was spread out underneath the court of King Minos in Crete and ate humans. Read this story about a brave and young prince, Theseus, who sets out to defeat the Minotaur.*

King Minos of Crete was a powerful man, feared by all the other rulers of the lands around him. When he demanded men for his great armies, they sent them without question. When he ordered them to send gifts to honour him, they felt they had no choice but to do as he said. It was the only way they could stop him from starting a war against them. But his orders to the nearby kingdom of Athens were the worst.

King Minos had a great palace. Under this palace, he had built a giant maze, a labyrinth, and at the centre of this maze, he kept a terrifying creature, the Minotaur. This was no ordinary animal; it was a monster, half man and half bull. The Minotaur was powerful and savage, and it loved to eat the humans who had been sent into the labyrinth by King Minos. These poor people would wander through the maze, completely lost, until at last they came face to face with the monster, who would then attack them.

savage: very cruel and violent

To keep his monster well fed, King Minos ordered that King Aegeus of Athens should send him seven young men and seven young women every year.

'Why do we send these young people to Crete every year?' young Prince Theseus asked his father, the King of Athens. 'And why is it that none of them ever return?'

'Because if we do not send them, Minos will wage war on us, and it is a war that we will not win,' said King Aegeus. 'And they do not return because they do not go to Crete as slaves. They go as food for the Minotaur.'

'Father, this is terrible!' shouted Theseus. 'We cannot let this go on. We cannot sacrifice any more of our young citizens to this tyrant. When it is time to send the next tribute, I will go as one of them, and I vow that it is the last time the Minotaur will be fed with any of our people.'

wage: carry out
tyrant: someone who treats others in a cruel and unfair way
vow: promise

discourage: try to convince someone not to do something
docked: a ship brought into the harbour
taunt: to say unkind or insulting things
humiliate: to make someone feel ashamed or foolish
jeered: made fun of or said rude things about someone loudly
puny: very small or weak
feeble: weak

His father tried to discourage him from going, but Theseus did not change his mind. King Aegeus reminded him that every year, other young men had sworn to kill this terrible beast, but they had never been seen again.

Theseus insisted that he understood the dangers but would succeed. 'I will return to you, Father,' cried Theseus, as the ship left the harbour wall, 'and you will be proud of your son.'

'Then I wish you good luck, my son,' said his father. 'I shall keep watch for you every day. If you are successful, take down these black sails, and replace them with white ones. That way I will know you are coming home safe to me.'

The next day, when Theseus' ship docked in Crete, King Minos himself came down to inspect the prisoners from Athens. He enjoyed the chance to taunt the Athenians and to humiliate them even further. 'Is this all your king has to offer this year?' he jeered. 'Such puny creatures. Hardly even a snack for the mighty creature within the labyrinth. Anyway, let's get on with it. I am not a hardhearted man, so I will let you choose which one goes first into the Minotaur's den. Who is it to be?'

Theseus stepped forward. 'I will go first. I am Theseus, Prince of Athens, and I do not fear what is within the walls of your maze.'

'Those are brave words for one so young and so feeble. But the Minotaur will soon have you between its horns,' replied King Minos. 'Guards! Open the labyrinth and send him in!'

Now the king didn't know that his daughter, Ariadne, was standing behind him, listening to everything. Hearing her father taunt the young prince, she decided that she would help him. When the prince entered the labyrinth and the guards walked away, she called softly to him.

'Theseus, take this,' she whispered.

'Even if you kill the Minotaur, you will never find your way out of the labyrinth without this.'

She threw him a great ball of string. Theseus tied one end of it to the entrance. He smiled at her, turned, and began to make his way into the maze, drawing the string behind him as he went.

Theseus walked carefully through the dark, foul-smelling passages of the labyrinth, expecting at any moment to come face-to-face with the creature. He did not have long to wait. Turning a corner, with his hands held out in front of him to feel his way, he suddenly touched what felt like a huge, bony horn.

In an instant, he was picked up between the Minotaur's horns and tossed high into the air. When he landed on the hard cold stone, he felt the animal's huge hooves come down on his chest. Every last breath seemed to be knocked out of him, and Theseus struggled to stay alive in the darkness.

But Theseus was no ordinary man. He was the son of a king. He was brave, and he was stubborn. As the Minotaur bellowed in his ear and grabbed at him with its hairy arms, Theseus grabbed the animal's huge horns, and kept on twisting the great head from side to side. As the animal grew weak, Theseus gave one almighty tug on the head, turning it almost right around. The creature's neck snapped, and it fell to the floor with an enormous thud.

It was over! He had done it! The Minotaur was dead. All Theseus had to do now was make his way out of... and then he realised the dreadful truth. In the struggle, he had let go of the string that would lead him out of the maze. He felt all over the floor in the pitch darkness and kept thinking he had found it, only to realise that all he had was a long wiry hair from the Minotaur.

Theseus wondered if this was where his life would end, down in the dark, all alone when his hand brushed a piece of string, and, with a cry of delight, he knew he had found the thread that would lead him

drawing: (here) pulling or dragging
hooves: (here) a bull's feet
struggled: tried hard to do something
dreadful: bad or very unpleasant
wiry: (here) rough to touch

back out. As he neared the entrance of the labyrinth, the darkness began to fade, and he could see Ariadne waiting for his return.

'You must take me back to Athens with you!' she cried. 'My father will kill me when he finds out that I have helped you!'

'Of course you must come with us,' said Theseus. 'It would be cruel to leave you here.' Quickly and quietly, they made their way to the prince's ship and set sail.

But in his haste to get away, Theseus forgot to change his sails to white. King Aegeus, who was waiting on the shores, saw the ship approaching with its black sails flying in the wind.

'My son has failed, and he is dead!' he cried. In despair, he flung himself from the cliff into the wild waters below. From that day on, the sea was named in memory of Theseus' father, and to this day, it is known as the Aegean Sea.

*(A Greek mythological tale)*

**despair:** the complete loss or absence of hope

## SUMMARY

Theseus, a brave Athenian prince, vows to kill the Minotaur, a monster. The Minotaur lived in Crete and every year the king of Athens was forced to send seven young men and women to be the monster's meal. That year Theseus goes to Crete along with others. He volunteers to enter the Minotaur's maze first. At the entrance, the princess of Crete, Ariadne, secretly hands over a ball of string to Theseus to help him find his way out of the dark maze. Fearless Theseus kills the Minotaur and emerges out of the maze. When Theseus had left for Crete, he had promised his father that he will change his ship's sails from black to white if he killed the Minotaur but he forgets to do so. On seeing the black sails, his father, King Aegeus, thinks that his son is dead. He is extremely upset by this and jumps into the sea.

### About the Genre

The word **mythology** is made from two Greek words: *mythos* meaning *story*, and *logy* meaning *to speak*. Hence, it means the telling of a story. Mythology is a collection of stories that usually deals with ancient history, beliefs, and customs of a certain culture.

## COMPREHENSION

**A. Read the descriptions and say whom/what they describe.**

1. He was a powerful king and a tyrant: ..........................
2. He was worried about his son. There is a sea named after him: ..........................
3. He was a young and brave boy. He tried to protect his people and set out to fight a monster: ..........................
4. She was a kind girl. She helped the prince find his way out of the maze: ..........................
5. He liked to eat humans. He was half bull and half man, and had big horns: ..........................
6. It was a large, dark area built under the palace. People would get lost in it. It was home to a monster: ..........................

**B. Read these sentences. Tick (✓) the correct sentences and cross (X) the incorrect ones.**

1. King Minos was a kind ruler. ☐
2. Athens had to agree to the demands made by King Minos to avoid war. ☐
3. King Minos asked for men and women to be sent as food for his monster. ☐
4. Aegeus readily agreed to send Theseus to Crete. ☐

5. Ariadne was a kind and thoughtful girl. ☐
6. King Aegeus jumped into the sea because he could not see the ship carrying his son. ☐

**C. Answer the questions briefly.**

1. Who was Minos? What kind of a man was he?
2. What were King Minos' order to the kingdom of Athens?
3. What did Aegeus ask Theseus to do while returning from Crete?
4. Describe how Theseus killed the Minotaur.
5. How did Ariadne help Theseus?

**D. Think and answer the questions.**

1. Theseus killed the Minotaur but lost his father. Do you think it's important to be brave as well as responsible? Give reasons for your answer.
2. Choose suitable adjectives for each of the characters in the story and complete the table.

*cruel* *honourable* *loving* *kind*
*brave* *clever* *hasty* *selfish*

| King Minos | King Aegeus | Theseus | Ariadne |
|---|---|---|---|
| | | | |
| | | | |

3. Talk to your partner/friend about your favourite character from the story and write a few lines about him/her.

## VOCABULARY

**The Minotaur is a mythological creature. Read the descriptions of some more mythological creatures, and label the pictures correctly. You may refer to the Internet or an encyclopedia.**

1. A **basilisk** is a reptile with the head of a cock, and wings. It can kill its enemies just by looking at them.

2. A **European dragon** is a reptile with wings.
   It breathes fire and guards treasure.
3. **Pegasus** is a horse with wings.
   It helps heroes in stories fight their enemies.
4. **Medusa** is a woman who has snakes on her head in place of hair.
   She can kill people just by looking at them.
5. A **unicorn** is a horse with a horn on its head.
6. A **phoenix** is a bird that burns itself and then is reborn from its own ashes.
7. **Hydra** is a huge water-snake-like monster with many heads, one of which is immortal. Every time one is cut off, two more heads grow.
8. **Cyclops** is a giant with an eye in the middle of his forehead.

a. ........................................

b. ........................................

c. ........................................

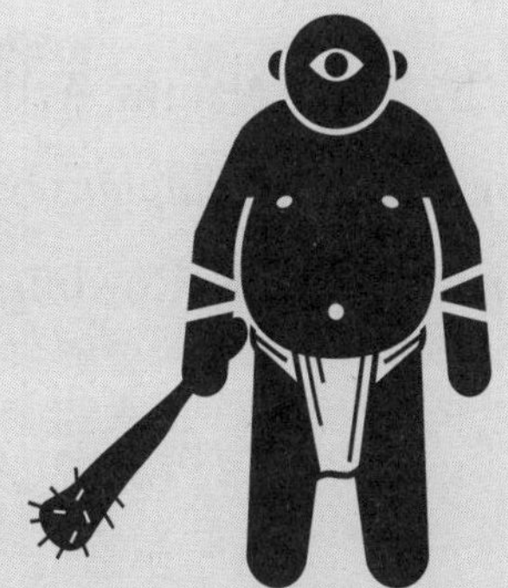

d. ........................................

e. ....................................

f. ....................................

g. ....................................

h. ....................................

*Read at leisure...*

- *Greek Myths* by Diane Namm, Arthur Pober, Eric Freeberg
- *Percy Jackson and the Olympians* by Rick Riordan
- *Harry Potter* series by J.K. Rowling

# 7 The Railway Children

## READING

*The three children—Peter, Phyllis and Bobbie decide to go pluck wild cherries near the mouth of a railway tunnel. Read on to find out what happens when they get there.*

'We'd better get down,' said Peter. 'I'm sure the cherries would be quite easy to get at from the side of the steps.' And they were almost at the gate when Bobbie said, 'Hush. Stop! What's that?'

'That' was a very odd noise indeed—a soft noise, but quite clearly heard through the sound of the wind in tree branches. It was a sort of whispering sound. As they listened it stopped, and then it began again.

And this time it did not stop, but it grew louder.

'Look'—cried Peter, suddenly—'the tree over there!'

The tree he pointed at was one of those that have rough grey leaves and white flowers. And, as Peter pointed, the tree was moving—not just the way trees should move when the wind blows through them, but all in one piece, as though it were a live creature and were walking down the side of the mountain.

'It's moving!' cried Bobbie.

'It's magic,' said Phyllis, breathlessly. 'I always knew this railway was enchanted.'

enchanted: magical

It really did seem a little like magic. For all the trees for about twenty yards of the opposite bank seemed to be slowly walking down towards the railway line like a flock of green sheep.

'What is it? Oh, what is it?' said Phyllis; 'it's much too magic for me. I don't like it. Let's go home.'

But Bobbie and Peter clung fast to the rail and watched excitedly. The trees moved on and on. Some stones and loose earth fell down and rattled on the railway metals far below.

'It's ALL coming down,' Peter tried to say, but he found there was hardly any voice to say it with. And, indeed, just as he spoke, the great rock, on the top of which the walking trees were, leaned slowly forward. The trees stopped walking, stood still, and shivered. Leaning with the rock, they seemed to hesitate a moment, and then rock and trees, and grass and bushes, with a rushing sound, slipped right away from the face of the mountain and fell on the railway line with a clumsy crash. A cloud of dust rose up.

'Look what a great heap it's made!' said Bobbie.

'Yes,' said Peter, slowly. He was still leaning on the fence. 'Yes,' he said again, still more slowly.

Then he stood upright.

'The 11:29 Down hasn't gone by yet. We must let them know at the station, or there'll be a most horrible accident.'

'Let's run,' said Bobbie, and began.

But Peter cried, 'Come back!' and looked at Mother's watch. He was very prompt and businesslike, and his face looked whiter than they had ever seen it.

'No time,' he said; 'it's two miles away, and it's past eleven.'

'Couldn't we,' suggested Phyllis, nervously, 'couldn't we climb up a telegraph post and do something to the wires?'

'We don't know how,' said Peter.

'They do it in war,' said Phyllis; 'I know I've heard of it.'

heap: an untidy pile of something
upright: straight
11:29 Down: a train that is due at 11:29 at the station
prompt: quick
miles: a distance of approximately 1.6 km

'They only CUT them, silly,' said Peter, 'and that doesn't do any good. And we couldn't cut them even if we got up. If we had anything red, we could get down on the line and wave it.'

'But the train wouldn't see us till it got round the corner, and then it could see the heap just as well as us,' said Phyllis; 'better, because it's much bigger than us.'

'If we only had something red,' Peter repeated, 'we could go round the corner and wave to the train.'

They got down the steep stairs. Bobbie was pale and shivering. Peter's face looked thinner than usual. Phyllis was red-faced with anxiety.

'Oh, how hot I am!' she said; 'and I thought it was going to be cold; I wish we hadn't put on our—' she stopped short—'our petticoats.'

'Oh, yes,' she cried; 'THEY'RE red! Let's take them off.'

They did, and with the petticoats rolled up under their arms, ran along the railway.
They ran at their best pace. Peter led, but the girls were not far behind. They reached the corner that hid the heap from the straight line of railway that ran half a mile without curve or corner.

'Now,' said Peter, taking hold of the largest flannel petticoat.

'You're not...' Phyllis hesitated, 'you're not going to TEAR them?'

'Be quiet,' said Peter, with harshness.

'Oh, yes,' said Bobbie, 'tear them into little bits if you like. Don't you see, Phyll, if we can't stop the train, there'll be a real live accident, with people KILLED. Oh, horrible!'

'There!' said Peter tearing the petticoat. He divided each petticoat into three pieces. 'Now, we've got six flags.' He looked at the watch again. 'And we've got seven minutes. We must have flagstaffs.'

The young saplings were broken off. Two came up by the roots. The leaves were stripped from them.

pale: almost white
petticoats: thin and loose skirts worn under dresses
flannel: a lightweight woollen fabric
flagstaffs: poles/sticks used to hold flags

'We must cut holes in the flags, and run the sticks through the holes,' said Peter. Two of the flags were set up in heaps of loose stones between the sleepers of the down line. Then Phyllis and Bobbie took each a flag, and stood ready to wave it as soon as the train came in sight.

'I shall have the other two myself,' said Peter, 'because it was my idea to wave something red.'

Perhaps Peter had not correctly calculated the number of minutes it would take the 11:29 to get from the station to the place where they were, or perhaps the train was late. Anyway, it seemed a very long time that they waited.

Phyllis grew impatient. It seemed to her that they had been standing there for hours and hours, holding those silly little red flags that no one would ever notice. The train wouldn't care. It would go rushing by them and tear round the corner and go crashing into that awful heap. But then came the distant rumble and hum of the metals, and a puff of white steam showed far away.

impatient: tired of waiting
rumble: a low continuous sound

'Stand firm,' said Peter, 'and wave like mad! When it gets to that big bush step back, but go on waving!'

The train came rattling along very, very fast.

'They don't see us! They won't see us! It's all no good!' cried Bobbie.

It seemed that the train came on as fast as ever. It was very near now.

'It's no good,' Bobbie said again.

'Stand back!' cried Peter, suddenly, and he dragged Phyllis back by the arm.

But Bobbie cried, 'Not yet, not yet!' and waved her flag right over

the line. The front of the engine looked black and enormous. Its voice was loud and harsh.

'Oh, stop, stop, stop!' cried Bobbie. No one heard her. But then it seemed as if the engine heard her—for it slowed swiftly, slowed and stopped, not twenty yards from the place where Bobbie's flag waved over the line. She saw the great black engine stop but somehow she could not stop waving the flag. And when the driver and the fireman had got off the engine and Peter and Phyllis had gone to meet them and pour out their excited tale of the awful heap just round the corner, Bobbie still waved the flag but more and more weakly.

When the others turned towards her she was lying across the line still gripping the stick of the little red flannel flag.

The engine-driver picked her up, carried her to the train, and laid her on the cushions of a first-class carriage.

'She has fainted,' he said, 'poor child. I'll just have a look at this heap and then we'll run you back to the station and get her seen to.'

They sat by Bobbie and the train ran back. Before it reached their station Bobbie had opened her eyes, and rolled herself over and begun to cry. And presently, when she stopped crying, they were able to laugh at her for being such a coward as to faint.

When the station was reached, the three were treated as heroes.

The praises they got for their 'prompt action,' and their 'common sense,' were enough to make anyone proud. Phyllis enjoyed herself thoroughly. She had never been a real heroine before, and the feeling was delicious.

Peter's ears got very red. Yet he, too, enjoyed himself. Only Bobbie wished they all wouldn't. She wanted to get away.

'Oh, come away, come away! I want to go home,' she said.

So they went. And as they went Station Master and Porter and guards and driver and fireman and passengers sent up a cheer.

'Oh, listen,' cried Phyllis; 'that's for US!'

'Yes,' said Peter. 'I say, I am glad I thought about something red, and waving it.'

'How lucky we DID put on our red petticoats!' said Phyllis.

'And it was US that saved them,' said Peter.

*(Taken from The Railway Children by E. Nesbit)*

## SUMMARY

Peter, Phyllis and Bobbie decide to pluck cherries from near the mouth of a railway tunnel. When they go there, they see trees moving down the side of the mountain and crash on the railway track. The children are worried because it was time for a train to arrive at that spot and there could be a horrible accident. The children decide to warn the engine driver and avoid the accident. They tear off their red petticoats and make flagstaffs out of it. They stand in wait for the train and wave their flags furiously when it arrives. The engine driver spots them just in time and stops the train. The brave children prevent a big accident and save lives.

## About the Author

**Edith Nesbit** (1858–1924) was a British poet, playwright, and children's author. It could be easily said that she was the first to write for children using adventure, fantasy, magic, and time travel. Some of her popular books are *Five Children and It, The New Treasure-Seekers* and *The Railway Children.*

# COMPREHENSION

**A. Fill in the blanks with the correct words from brackets.**

1. The children went to pluck .................................. (*berries/cherries*) from the mountain side.
2. The children heard the .................................. (*train whistle/rumble of trees*).
3. They thought they saw the .................................. (*mountain/trees*) moving.
4. .................................. (*Phyllis/Bobbie*) was scared and wanted to go home.
5. The rocks fell in a heap on the .................................. (*railway line/fence*).

6. The children decided to make flags from their .................................... (*frocks/petticoats*).

7. The children made flagstaffs from .................................... (*trees/saplings*).

8. .................................... (*Peter/Bobbie*) continued to wave the flag even after the train stopped.

**B. Answer the questions briefly.**

1. Who went to pluck cherries?
2. What did the children see?
3. What were the children scared of?
4. Why did the children not inform the station about the heap of stones?
5. How did the children decide to avoid the crash of the train?
6. Describe how the children made the flags.
7. How were the children treated at the station? Do you think they deserved it? Give a reason.

**C. Think and answer the questions.**

1. The children's timely reaction avoided a big accident. Comment on this statement.
2. Why do you think Bobbie faints after the train stops?
3. When the children saw the rocks falling, they got scared. However, they decided to do something to avoid an accident. What does this tell you about the children?

## VOCABULARY

**Analogy**

- An **analogy** is a comparison between one thing and another.
- It is usually used for the purpose of explanation or clarification.
  For example:

  *Many is to few as together is to alone.*

  *Sing is to sang as eat is to ate.*

**A. Choose the correct word to end each sentence. One has been done for you.**

1. North is to south as polite is to .........*rude*......... (*friendly/rude*).

2. Patient is to impatient as excited is to .................................... (*breathless/nervous*).

3. Less is to more as lazy is to ...................................... (*active/sleepy*).

4. Enormous is to tiny as late is to ...................................... (*lazy/prompt*).

5. Heavy is to light as gentle is to ...................................... (*rough/soft*).

6. Awful is to unpleasant as heroic is to ...................................... (*cowardly/brave*).

7. Smart is to intelligent as sly is to ...................................... (*genius/sneaky*).

8. Which is to witch as weather is to ...................................... (*whether/wither*).

**B. Complete these railway words with the help of the given clues.**

1. The length of the space covered by a vehicle between two stations: DI ... ... ... ... ... ...
2. It is a system of transport in which small trains travel along a single rail which is usually high above the ground: MO ... ... ... ... ... ...
3. A person travelling in a train: PA ... ... ... ... ... ... ...
4. A passage made through a hill: TU ... ... ... ...
5. A building by the railway line where the train stops: ST ... ... ... ... ...
6. A place where railway lines join: JU... ... ... ... ... ...
7. An area beside the rails where you wait for or get off a train: PL ... ... ... ... ... ...
8. The pair of long metal bars a train travels along: TR ... ... ...

*Read at leisure...*

- *Five Children and It* by E. Nesbit
- *The Wonderful Wizard of Oz* by L. Frank Baum
- *The Lion, the Witch and the Wardrobe* by C.S. Lewis

# 8 The Fisherman

## READING

*Have you ever seen fishermen? Do you wonder what their lives are like? Are they similar to us or different than us? Read this poem to find out more about fishermen.*

**Literary device**

**Simile** is the use of the word *like* or *as* to compare the qualities of two people or things. The following lines in the poem use simile.

*They're like the sea on foggy days.*

*They're like the wondrous tales he tells.*

The fisherman goes out at dawn
When every one's abed,
And from the bottom of the sea
Draws up his daily bread.

His life is strange; half on the shore
And half upon the sea—
Not quite a fish, and yet not quite
The same as you and me.

The fisherman has curious eyes;
They make you feel so queer,
As if they had seen many things
Of wonder and of fear.

dawn: that time of day when light first appears in the sky, just before the sun rises
abed: (old English) in bed
queer: strange

They're like the sea on foggy days,—
Not gray, nor yet quite blue;
They're like the wondrous tales he tells
Not quite—yet maybe—true.

He knows so much of boats and tides,
Of winds and clouds and sky!
But when I tell of city things,
He sniffs and shuts one eye!

*–Abbie Farwell Brown*

**tides:** currents in the sea that are caused by the regular and continuous movement of large areas of water towards and away from the shore

## SUMMARY

The poem talks about the life of a fisherman. He works when everyone is still in bed and earns his living by fishing. The poet compares the life of a fisherman to that of someone who spends half his time in water and the other half on land. He wonders about the many strange things that the fisherman may have seen, and though the fisherman knows everything about the sea, he shows no interest when the poet tells him about cities.

## About the Poet

**Abbie Farwell Brown** (1871–1927) was an American poet. Brown started writing when still at school and was also one of the founders of her school newspaper, *The Jabberwock*. The newspaper is still being published by the school and is one of the oldest newspapers in the United States. Brown published her first children's book, *The Book of Saints and Friendly Beasts,* in 1900. In addition to stories, Brown also produced poetry for children.

## COMPREHENSION

**A. Mark the sentences as true (T) or false (F).**

1. The fisherman goes fishing when everyone is still in bed. ☐
2. The fisherman catches fish every day. ☐
3. The poet finds the fisherman's life difficult to understand. ☐
4. The fisherman does not know much about boats. ☐
5. The fisherman likes listening about life in the city. ☐

**B. Read the poem again. Fill in the word web with words related to the fisherman.**

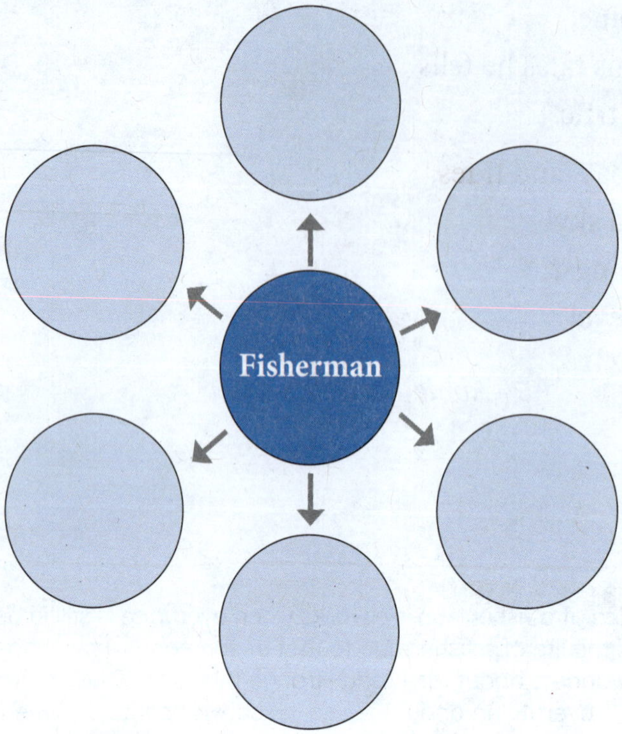


**C. Read these lines from the poem and answer the questions.**

1. *The fisherman has curious eyes;*
   *They make you feel so queer,*
   *As if they had seen many things*
   *Of wonder and of fear.*

   a. Why does the poet call the fisherman's eyes *curious*?
   b. What kind of things do you think the fisherman has seen?

2. *They're like the sea on foggy days,—*
   *Not gray, nor yet quite blue;*
   *They're like the wondrous tales he tells*
   *Not quite—yet maybe—true.*

   a. What is like the sea on foggy days?
   b. Why does the poet make this comparison?
   c. What do you think the poet wanted to say after 'Not quite…'?
   d. Why does the poet call the tales *wondrous*?

**D. Think and answer the questions.**

1. The poet calls the life of the fisherman *strange*. Why does she say so? Do you think so too? Give a reason for your answer.

2. Why does the fisherman *sniff* when he hears about city things? What do you think he feels about city life?
3. Find two pairs of rhyming words in the poem.
4. Imagine the fisherman told you a *wondrous tale*. Write it down and read it out in the class.
5. Do you like the character of the fisherman in the poem? What do you like/dislike about him? Give reasons for your answer.

## VOCABULARY

**Use the following similes in sentences of your own. One has been done for you.**

1. Light as a feather

   *On Wednesdays, we don't have to carry many books, so my bag is light as a feather.*
2. Blind as a bat
3. Tough as nails
4. Hard as rock
5. Fierce like a tiger
6. Sleep like a baby
7. Easy as a pie
8. Like a fish

*Read at leisure...*

- *Friends* by Abbie Farwell Brown
- *Paper Boats* by Rabindranath Tagore
- *Boats Sail on the Rivers* by Christina Rossetti

# 9 First Day on the Mountain

## READING

HC

*Heidi, a little girl of about six years of age, has lost both her parents. Her aunt, Dete, cannot keep Heidi with her anymore. So she brings Heidi to live with her grandfather, who lives alone on a mountain. Grandfather is known to be a grumpy old man. Read on to find out what happens next.*

As soon as Dete had disappeared, the old man went back to his bench, and there he remained seated, staring at the ground without uttering a sound.

Heidi, meanwhile, was enjoying herself in her new surroundings; she looked about till she found a shed where the goats were kept. She peeped in, and saw it was empty. She continued her search and came to the fir trees behind the hut. A strong breeze was blowing through them. Heidi stood still and listened. The sound growing fainter, she went on again, to the other corner of the hut, and so around to where her grandfather was sitting. He was in exactly the same position as when she had left him.

She went and placed herself in front of the old man, and putting her hands behind her back, stood and gazed at him. 'What is it you want?' he asked.

'I want to see what you have inside the house,' said Heidi.

'Come then!' And the grandfather rose and went towards the hut.

fainter: (here) not as loud as before

'Bring your bundle of clothes in with you,' he told her.

'I shan't want them anymore,' was her prompt answer.

'And why shall you not want them anymore?' he asked.

'Because I want to go about like the goats with their thin light legs.'

'Well, you can do so if you like,' said her grandfather, 'but bring the things in, we must put them in the cupboard.'

Heidi did as she was told. The old man now opened the door, and Heidi stepped inside after him. She found herself in a good-sized room, which covered the whole ground floor of the hut. A table and a chair were the only furniture; in one corner stood the grandfather's bed, and on the further side was a large door in the wall—this was the cupboard. The grandfather opened it. It had everything that grandfather needed for his food and clothing. As soon as it was opened, Heidi ran forward and thrust in her bundle of clothes, far back behind her grandfather's things, so that they might not easily be found again. She then looked carefully round the room, and asked, 'Where am I to sleep, Grandfather?'

'Wherever you like,' he answered.

prompt: quick

Heidi was delighted, and began to examine all the nooks and corners to find out where it would be pleasantest to sleep.

In the corner near her grandfather's bed, she saw a short ladder against the wall. Up she climbed and found herself in the hayloft.

hayloft: a place used for storing hay
to and fro: move repeatedly from one place to another and back again
rummaging: searching for something by moving things around hurriedly
coarse: rough

There lay a large heap of fresh sweet-smelling hay; while through a round window in the wall, she could see right down to the valley.

'I shall sleep up here, Grandfather. It's lovely up here. Come up and see how lovely it is!' she called down to him.

'Oh, I know all about it,' he called up in answer.

'I am getting the bed ready now,' she called down again, as she went busily to and fro at her work, 'but I shall want you to bring me up a sheet.'

'All right,' said the grandfather, and he went to the cupboard, and after rummaging about inside for a few minutes, he drew out a long, coarse piece of cloth, which was all he had. He carried it up to the loft, where he found that Heidi had already made quite a nice bed. She had put an extra heap of hay at one end for a pillow, and so arranged it that, when in bed, she would be able to see comfortably out through the round window.

The two together now spread the sheet over the bed. It looked now as tidy and comfortable a bed as you could wish for.

'I think we might have something to eat now,' said the grandfather. 'What do you think?'

Heidi was terribly hungry, so she answered without hesitation, 'Yes, I think so too.'

'Let us go down then,' said the old man.

Grandfather then went up to the fireplace, pushed the big kettle aside, and drew forward the little one that was hanging on the chain, and seating himself on a stool before the fire, blew it up into a clear bright flame. The kettle soon began to boil, and meanwhile the old man held a large piece of cheese on a long iron fork over the fire, turning it round and round till it was toasted a nice golden yellow colour on each side. Heidi watched all that was going on with eager curiosity. Suddenly, some new idea seemed to come into her head, for she turned and ran to the cupboard, and then began going busily backwards and forwards.

Soon the grandfather got up and came to the table with a jug and the cheese, and there he saw it already tidily laid, with the round loaf and two plates and two knives each in its right place; for Heidi had taken exact note that morning of all that there was in the cupboard, and she knew which things would be wanted for their meal.

'Ah, that's right,' said the grandfather, 'I am glad to see that you have some ideas of your own.' And as he spoke, he laid the food on the table. 'But what will you do for a seat?'

The grandfather himself was sitting on the only chair in the room. Heidi flew to the fireplace, and dragging the stool up to the table, sat herself down upon it.

'Well, you have found a seat for yourself, but a low one, I see,' said the grandfather.

He then stood up, filled the bowl with milk, and placing it on the chair, pushed it in front of Heidi. He brought her a large slice of bread and a piece of the golden cheese, and told her to eat. Heidi lifted the bowl with both hands and drank without pause till it was empty.

'Was the milk nice?' asked her grandfather.

'I never drank any so good before,' answered Heidi.

Once the meal got over, the grandfather went outside to put the goat-shed in order. Then he went to the little well-shed, and there he cut some long round sticks, and a small round board; in this he bored some holes and stuck the sticks into them, and there, as if made by

flew: (here) moved fast
bored: drilled

speechless: not able to speak, usually because of shock or surprise
midst: in the middle

magic, was a three-legged stool just like her grandfather's, only higher. Heidi stood and looked at it, speechless with astonishment.

'What do you think that is?' asked her grandfather.

'It's my stool, I know, because it is such a high one; and it was made in all of a minute,' said the child, still lost in wonder and admiration.

The grandfather continued working in the shed, mending whatever was needed. Heidi followed him step by step, her eyes attentively taking in all that he did, and everything that she saw was a fresh source of pleasure to her. And so the time passed happily on till evening. Suddenly, a shrill whistle was heard. Grandfather came out. Down from the heights above, a herd of goats came springing one after another, with Peter in their midst. Two of the goats ran to where the grandfather was standing.

Heidi tenderly stroked the two goats in turn, running first to one side of them, and then the other, jumping about in her glee at the pretty little animals. 'Are they ours, Grandfather? Are they both ours? Are you going to put them in the shed? Will they always stay with us?'

Heidi's questions came tumbling out one after the other so that her grandfather had only time to answer each of them with, 'Yes, yes.' Grandfather told her to go and fetch her bowl and the bread. Heidi obeyed and was soon back again. The grandfather milked the white goat and filled her basin, and broke off a piece of bread. 'Now eat your supper,' he said, 'and then go up to bed.'

Not long after, and while it was still twilight, the grandfather also went to bed, for he was up every morning at sunrise.

During the night, a strong mountain wind blew so strong that the hut trembled and the old beams groaned and creaked.

'The child will be frightened,' the grandfather murmured half aloud. He mounted the ladder and went and stood by the child's bed.

Heidi lay under the heavy coverlid, her cheeks rosy with sleep, her head peacefully resting on her little round arm, and with a happy expression on her baby face, as if dreaming of something pleasant. The old man stood looking down on the sleeping child until the moon again disappeared behind the clouds and he could see no more. Then he went back to bed.

*(Extracted and abridged from Heidi by Johanna Spyri)*

**glee:** a feeling of happiness and excitement
**twilight:** the time just before night when the daylight has almost gone, but when it is not completely dark
**mounted:** climbed up

## SUMMARY

Heidi, a six-year-old girl, has lost both her parents. Her Aunt Dete brings her to live with her grandfather. Her grandfather lives alone in a hut on the top of a mountain. On her first day with her grandfather, Heidi makes her bed in the hayloft from where she can see the stars in the sky. She enjoys eating a meal of cheese, bread, and milk with her grandfather. He makes her a special stool to sit on and she also plays with his goats. Heidi has a great first day on the mountain.

## About the Author

**Johanna Louise Spyri** (1827–1901) was a Swiss author. She was known to write stories that talk about childish joys and sorrows. Her best work, *Heidi*, is a book for children, and is popular all over the world.

## COMPREHENSION

**A. Heidi does many things on her first day on the mountain. Put all of them in the correct sequence.**

1. Heidi makes her bed in the hayloft. ☐
2. Heidi goes to bed in her hayloft. ☐
3. Heidi hides her clothes in the cupboard. ☐
4. Heidi greets the goats. ☐
5. Heidi lays the table for lunch. ☐
6. Grandfather and Heidi eat supper. ☐

**B. Choose the correct option.**

1. Heidi hides her clothes in the cupboard because
   a. she doesn't feel cold.
   b. she wants to be free like the goats.
   c. Grandfather gave her new clothes to wear.
2. Grandfather made a stool for Heidi because
   a. Heidi asked him for a new stool.
   b. there was nothing for Heidi to sit on.
   c. the only stool he had was too low for her.
3. Grandfather and Heidi go to bed
   a. in the afternoon.
   b. when the sun begins to set.
   c. very late in the night.

**C. Answer the questions briefly.**

1. Where does the grandfather live, and with whom?
2. How and where does Heidi prepare her bed?
3. What does Heidi eat at her grandfather's house? Does she enjoy her meal?
4. Why does the grandfather wake up in the middle of the night to see Heidi?
5. Write four qualities of Heidi that you can think of.

**D. Think and answer the questions.**

1. Heidi makes her bed in the hayloft. Would you also wish to sleep in a similar bed each night? Why/Why not?
2. What kind of a person is the grandfather? Give examples from the story to support your answer.
3. Heidi and her grandfather share a pleasant relationship. Write about your relationship with your grandparent(s). You could talk about what you like about them, what you do together, and what you have learnt from them.
4. You read about Heidi's first day on the mountain. Fill in the table given below to say what you think she does the next day. One has been done for you.

| | |
|---|---|
| 6:00 a.m. | *Heidi wakes up early to help her grandfather milk the goats.* |
| 7:00 a.m. | |
| 8:00 a.m. | |
| 11:00 a.m. | |
| 1:00 p.m. | |
| 4:00 p.m. | |
| 5:00 p.m. | |
| 7:00 p.m. | |

# VOCABULARY

## Movement words

There are many different words that show movement. For example:

*Heidi flew to the fireplace.*

Here, *flew* means she *ran quickly*.

**A. Underline the words the author uses to talk about movement in these sentences.**

1. Heidi sprang forward with a cry of joy and rushed to greet the goats.
2. He carried it up to the loft, where he found that Heidi had already made quite a nice bed.
3. As soon as he opened the cupboard, Heidi ran towards it and thrust in her bundle of clothes.

**B. Complete these sentences with the movement words from the box. Use a dictionary if required.**

*marched*   *slithered*   *mounted*   *chased*   *bounced*   *tiptoed*

1. The ball .......................................... down the hill and got lost in the bushes.
2. Grandfather .......................................... the stairs to look at Heidi.
3. The police .......................................... the thieves in the streets.
4. The green snake .......................................... through the wet grass.
5. The soldiers .......................................... proudly in the parade.
6. We slipped out of our beds and .......................................... to the kitchen in the night.

*Read at leisure...*

- *Matilda* by Roald Dahl
- *The Little Prince* by Antoine de Saint-Exupéry
- *The Secret Garden* by Frances Hodgson Burnett

# 10 The Little Land

15 LIFE ON LAND

## READING

*What do you dream of at night? Have you ever dreamt of magical places and people, or of doing things that no one else could? Read on to find out what the poet imagines doing when he shuts his eyes.*

When at home alone I sit  
And am very tired of it,  
I have just to shut my eyes  
To go sailing through the skies—  
To go sailing far away  
To the pleasant Land of Play;  
To the fairy land afar  
Where the Little People are;  
Where the clover-tops are trees,  
And the rain-pools are the seas,  
And the leaves, like little ships,  
Sail about on tiny trips;  
And above the Daisy tree  
Through the grasses,  
High o'erhead the Bumble Bee  
Hums and passes.

**clover:** a small plant with pink or white, ball-shaped flowers

In that forest to and fro
I can wander, I can go;
See the spider and the fly,
And the ants go marching by,
Carrying parcels with their feet
Down the green and grassy street.
I can in the sorrel sit
Where the ladybird alit.
I can climb the jointed grass
And on high
See the greater swallows pass
In the sky,
And the round sun rolling by
Heeding no such things as I.

Through that forest I can pass
Till, as in a looking-glass,
Humming fly and daisy tree
And my tiny self I see,
Painted very clear and neat
On the rain-pool at my feet.
Should a leaflet come to land
Drifting near to where I stand,
Straight I'll board that tiny boat
Round the rain-pool sea to float.

Little thoughtful creatures sit
On the grassy coasts of it;
Little things with lovely eyes
See me sailing with surprise.
Some are clad in armour green—
(These have sure to battle been!)—
Some are pied with ev'ry hue,

**Literary device**

Remember what alliteration is? **Alliteration** occurs when words beginning with the same letter or sound appear together or close to each other. The following expressions in the poem are examples of alliteration.

*on tiny trips*

*green and grassy street*

*round sun rolling by*

**sorrel:** a plant whose leaves have a bitter taste
**alit:** (past form of *alight*) to land
**heeding:** paying attention to
**armour:** special metal clothing that soldiers wore for protection in battle in olden times

Black and crimson, gold and blue;
Some have wings and swift are gone;
But they all look kindly on.

When my eyes I once again
Open, and see all things plain:
High bare walls, great bare floor;
Great big knobs on drawer and door;
Great big people perched on chairs,
Stitching tucks and mending tears,
Each a hill that I could climb,
And talking nonsense all the time—
O dear me,
That I could be
A sailor on a the rain-pool sea,
A climber in the clover tree,
And just come back a sleepy-head,
Late at night to go to bed.

*–R.L. Stevenson*

knobs: round handles on a door or drawer used to open or close it
perched: (here) sat
tucks: (here) folds or pleats in a garment

## SUMMARY

The poem talks about the fantastic land of imagination of the poet's dreams. When he is tired, the poet closes his eyes and imagines himself to be in a 'Land of play' with fairy people, beautiful creatures, faraway forests, and pools of clear water. This world of his dreams is very beautiful. Although when he wakes up, he finds himself back in his ordinary room. He wishes that he could be a sailor or a climber who just comes back to his plain life to go to bed.

### About the Poet

**Robert Louis Stevenson** (1850–1894) was a famous Scottish writer, and came from a wealthy family. His most popular book, *Treasure Island*, was first published in 1883. It was quite successful and turned him into a well-known writer. Unfortunately, Robert suffered from poor health since childhood. His illness continued in his adulthood, and much of his writing was done from his sickbed. In 1886, he wrote two novels, *The Strange Case of Dr Jekyll and Mr Hyde* and *Kidnapped*, which were also well received.

## COMPREHENSION

**A. Answer the questions briefly.**

1. Where does the poet imagine going when he shuts his eyes?
2. Mention any two things the poet dreams of doing.
3. What will the poet do with the leaflet?
4. Who do you think are the creatures in *armour green*?
5. What does the poet see when he opens his eyes? Does he like what he sees?
6. What do you think the poet means by the following?
   a. *sailing through the skies*
   b. *grassy coasts*

**B. Read these lines from the poem and answer the questions.**

1. *When at home alone I sit*
   *And am very tired of it,*
   *I have just to shut my eyes*
   *To go sailing through the skies—*

   a. What does the poet do when he is alone?
   b. What do you think he is tired of?
   c. What does the poet imagine when he shuts his eyes?

2. *See the greater swallows pass*
*In the sky,*
*And the round sun rolling by*
*Heeding no such things as I.*

   a. What will the poet see in the Land of Play?

   b. Why do you think the sun does not notice the poet?

3. *Great big people perched on chairs,*
*Stitching tucks and mending tears,*
*Each a hill that I could climb,*
*And talking nonsense all the time—*

   a. Who are the *great big people*?

   b. What are these people doing?

   c. Is the poet happy to see them?

   d. Why do you think he says *big people* talk nonsense?

## C. Think and answer the questions.

1. Write about a place you cannot wait to visit. It could be either a real place or an imaginary one.

2. With the help of your partner, make a list of all the things the poet would see and do when he visits the Land of Play. One of each has been done for you.

| Things he'd see | Things he'd do |
|---|---|
| *Ships made of leaves* | *Wander in the forest* |
| | |
| | |
| | |
| | |

3. The poet has made use of beautiful words and images to make the poem more realistic. Read these lines from the poem and draw a picture that comes to your mind. Colour the picture.

*Where the Little People are;*
*Where the clover-tops are trees,*
*And the rain-pools are the seas,*
*And the leaves, like little ships,*
*Sail about on tiny trips;*
*And above the Daisy tree*
*Through the grasses,*
*High o'erhead the Bumble Bee*
*Hums and passes.*

## VOCABULARY

### Alliteration

Read these examples of alliteration.

*Lazy lizards are leaping like frogs.*

*Round and round the rabbit ran.*

*A big bug bit my finger.*

**A. Read these sentences and underline the alliteration used in each of them.**

1. Pooja picked a peculiar pen from the floor.
2. Krish called me to ask about his craft kit.
3. Cherry chose a comfortable chair in class.
4. Betty bought some butter from the baker.
5. Frenny and her friends had fun at the fair.

**B. Form sentences using alliteration with the sounds *s*, *f*, and *sh*.**

**C. Read these famous tongue twisters.**

INDIA FOCUS

1. How much wood would a woodchuck chuck if a woodchuck could chuck wood?
2. Frivolously fanciful Fannie fried fresh fish furiously.

**Think of at least two tongue twisters in your mother tongue. Share them with your friends. Translate, if necessary.**

*Read at leisure...*

- *From a Railway Carriage* by R.L. Stevenson
- *Foreign Lands* by R.L. Stevenson
- *Travel* by Edna St Vincent Millay

# Notes

# Notes

# Notes